LAKE HURON

A TRUE BOOK

by

Ann Armbruster

Plano Community Library District
15 N. Center Ave.
Plano, IL 60545

 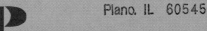

Children's Press®
A Division of Grolier Publishing

New York London Hong Kong Sydney
Danbury, Connecticut

Reading Consultant
Linda Cornwell
*Learning Resource Consultant
Indiana Department of
Education*

Subject Consultant
William D. Ellis
*Editor of the quarterly journal
of the Great Lakes
Historical Society*

Children enjoy a hayride
along Lake Huron.

Library of Congress Cataloging-in-Publication Data

Armbruster, Ann.
  Lake Huron/by Ann Armbruster.
    p.   cm. — (A true book)
  Includes index.
  Summary: Discusses the history, nautical stories, and industrial and
social significance of Lake Huron.
  ISBN 0-516-20012-7 (lib. bdg.)   ISBN 0-516-26103-7 (pbk.)
  1. Huron, Lake (Mich. and Ont.)—Juvenile literature. [1. Huron, Lake
(Mich. and Ont.)] I. Title. II. Series.
F554.A76 1996
977.4—dc20   96-2026
                                                                 CIP
                                                                  AC

14
10/2013

Contents

Thousands of years ago, glaciers carved out the Great Lakes.

The Second-Largest Lake

Thousands of years ago, glaciers covered much of North America. The glaciers moved down slowly from the North. They carved deep grooves in the earth. When they melted, the water formed lakes and rivers in the lower lands.

A
D
A

GULF OF
ST. LAWRENCE

QUEBEC

Prince
Edward
Island

St. Lawrence River

New
Brunswick

Montreal

Maine

Nova Scotia

RIO

Vermont

New
Hampshire

New York

Massachusetts

Connecticut

Rhode
Island

TES

New Jersey

ATLANTIC
OCEAN

The five Great Lakes—Lake Erie, Lake Huron, Lake Michigan, Lake Ontario, and Lake Superior—are a result of this glacial period.

Lake Huron is the second-largest of the Great Lakes. Rivers and canals connect Lake Huron to Lake Erie, Lake Michigan, and Lake Superior.

The Huron Indians

American Indians were the first people to live around Lake Huron. The Iroquois, the Algonquin, and the Wendat Indians fished and hunted there. Many people believe they originally came from Asia, walking across a land bridge over the Bering Sea.

The American Indians' best resource was the land.

When French explorers met some Wendat Indians, they called them the *Huron*. In French, the word *huron* means "rough" and "untidy." The French called the area where the Indians lived *Huronia*.

Huron Culture

The Huron lived in towns and villages. They built large log houses, called longhouses, in regular rows. Many Huron families lived in each long-house. One longhouse was home for up to twenty-four women of the same clan. Each woman had her own husband and children. When

A longhouse held many Huron families.

a man married, he moved into
his wife's longhouse.

Each village also had a
council house. The Huron
used this house for meetings.

The Huron had some very
democratic ideas. They believed
that all people had the right to

make decisions for themselves. If children misbehaved, adults patiently corrected them instead of punishing them.

The Huron raised corn, beans, and squash. The men hunted and cleared the fields of trees and brush. The women planted crops.

American Indian women gather wild rice.

Hurons made clothing from animal skins. They often traded the skins for other goods.

With the arrival of the French in Montreal, Canada, the fur trade developed. In Montreal, the Huron came in contact with European people who had diseases that were unknown in North America. Smallpox and measles swept through the Huron, bringing sickness and death.

These diseases caused confusion and bitterness. Often

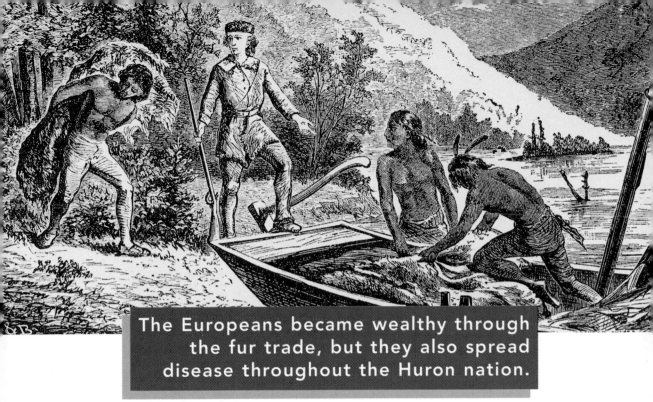

The Europeans became wealthy through the fur trade, but they also spread disease throughout the Huron nation.

entire families died. American Indians had no defense.

In 1634, twenty thousand Indians lived in Huronia. By 1640, only ten thousand were left.

Later, the Huron were forced to move from place to place. They became a divided people.

Explorers and Traders

In the early 1500s, European nations were seeking a "Northwest Passage"—a water route to China. Stories were told of great riches in Asia. The English, Spanish, and Portuguese had explored lands in the Americas.

In 1535, France sent Jacques Cartier to North

America, where he sailed the St. Lawrence River. He also discovered rich natural resources, such as copper, quartz, and a large beaver population.

American Indians (above) and Canadian fur traders (far right) trapped beavers (right) for trade.

Beaver coats and hats were popular in Europe. They brought high prices. The land

and forests around Lake Huron were rich in beavers.

As Cartier explored the St. Lawrence River, he met American-Indian hunters. The Indians were eager to trade animal skins, which the French could ship back to Europe.

Trade soon developed between the French and the Indians. Indians traded beaver skins for cooking pots, knives, and tools.

Iron pots and tools became treasured items. They lasted

longer than those the Indians made from clay.

In 1615, Samuel de Champlain, a French explorer, sailed on a lake he named La Mer Douce, (Freshwater Sea). The lake was later named Lake Huron for the Huron Indians who lived nearby.

These exchanges between explorers and American Indians were the beginning of the fur trade. It continued for nearly three hundred years.

Samuel de Champlain (above) sailed Lake Huron in the 1600s. A statue of Champlain stands in Quebec today (right).

The Northwest Passage

Many explorers spent their lives trying to find a northwest passage that would create a faster trade route to the riches in Asia. John Cabot of Britain was the first to try in 1497, then came Giovanni da Verrazano (1524) of Italy and Jacques Cartier (1534) of France.

Other explorers followed. They found that the route was not via the Great Lakes, but by a series of channels through Canada's Arctic Islands. It took centuries until this route was conquered. In 1906, **the Norwegian explorer Roald Amundsen** completed the three-year journey, and was the first person to successfully navigate the Northwest Passage.

The search for the Northwest Passage has been called **one of the world's most dangerous maritime journeys.**

The Voyageurs

By the early 1700s, the French controlled the Great Lakes fur trade. They transported goods on waterways by canoe. The canoes were made of birch bark, cedar strips, and pine gum. Most of them weighed about 300 pounds (136 kilograms) and often hauled tons of men and cargo.

Voyageurs traveled the waterways by canoe.

Men called voyageurs pad-
dled the canoes. *Voyageur* is
a French word meaning "trav-
eler." They were a hardy and
colorful group. Voyageurs

The canoes were made of bark and pine gum.

could paddle for countless hours. They were short men with powerful arms and shoulders—tall men could not fit in the canoes!

Voyageurs were also called *mangeurs de lard*, a French phrase meaning "pork eaters." Their daily meal was a piece of pork with dried corn or peas.

Voyageurs measured the distances they traveled in "pipes." Pipes referred to the number of smoking breaks during a trip. After paddling for a certain time, voyageurs

Today, people reenact voyageur journeys of the past.

Voyageurs settled in camps at night.

stopped to rest and smoke their clay pipes. A short journey might be a twenty-pipe trip. A long one could be a hundred-pipe trip!

The Griffon

The *Griffon* was the first sailing ship built on the Great Lakes. In 1679, René Robert Cavelier, Sieur de La Salle launched the ship on the Niagara River. The *Griffon* was small compared to today's ships. It was 60 feet (18 meters) long and weighed 45 tons (41 metric tons).

Robert Cavelier, Sieur de La Salle (left), launched the *Griffon* on the Great Lakes. It was the first ship built in North America for exploration (above).

The *Griffon* sailed the length of Lake Erie in three days. Then it sailed up Lake Huron toward Mackinac Island. On Lake Huron, the tiny ship survived a furious storm. Then, from the

The *Griffon* rides the Great Lakes.

Straits of Mackinac, it sailed to Green Bay, Wisconsin.

On its long return voyage, The *Griffon* vanished. Many people believe the ship sank in a storm on Lake Huron.

THE GREAT STORM OF 1913

In November, Great Lakes weather turns wild and unpredictable. Storms appear in a matter of minutes. Back in 1913, old sailors said it would be an unlucky year. They were right.

On November 7, 1913, a violent storm struck the Great Lakes with no warning. Ships were lost on all the Great Lakes that night. Lighthouse beacons showed the way to safe harbors, but most ships were unable to reach them. Monstrous waves chewed up dozens of ships.

On Lake Huron, eight large freighters disappeared without a trace. The crewmen and 178 passengers were lost.

The Straits of Mackinac

A strait is a narrow strip of water between two larger bodies of water. The Straits of Mackinac connect Lake Huron and Lake Michigan. They separate Upper and Lower Michigan.

At first, people crossed the Straits of Mackinac in canoes. In the 1800s, railroads were built up to the straits.

33

Transportation stopped at the narrow passage. Later, ferryboats called railroad ferries rode the straits. They hauled barges loaded with railroad cars.

After the automobile was invented, people began driving to the straits. Car ferries were

Cars line up to load the ferry (above) and then cross the Straits of Mackinac (left).

built to carry the cars across. These ferries had openings at both ends. Cars could drive in one end and out the other.

Soon there were more and more cars, and more and more people. Some people thought about building a bridge across the straits.

Big Mac

A lot of people said the idea of a bridge was impossible. No bridge could stand up to the grinding ice and the strong winds. But the engineers said it could be done.

The 5-mile-(8-kilometer-) long Mackinac Bridge was completed in 1957. Sometimes called

Construction of Big Mac

Big Mac, it is an engineering marvel. At its center, the bridge is 199 feet (61 m) above the water. As cars drive over the bridge, huge ships pass underneath it.

Huge ships can now travel under the bridge.

Big Mac is the world's longest, costliest, and safest bridge. Michigan is no longer a divided state.

Mackinac Island

Lake Huron and Lake Michigan can both be seen from Mackinac Island. No cars are allowed there. The environment of the 1800s is quietly preserved.

Mackinac Island lies at the entrance to the Straits of Mackinac. It is heavily wooded and scenic and a popular summer resort.

Mackinac Island has beautiful views. No cars are allowed on the island, so people ride bicycles instead (bottom).

Many historic events happened there. In the 1600s, it was the center of French missionary activity among the American Indians. The British later seized the island. In the 1800s, John Jacob Astor established the American Fur Company on Mackinac Island.

John Jacob Astor

Lake Huron Today

Lake Huron acts as a bridge within the Great Lakes system. It is a connecting waterway to the other Great Lakes. The Detroit and St. Clair rivers connect it to Lake Erie. The Straits of Mackinac connect it to Lake Michigan.

Lake Huron has more islands than the other Great Lakes.

Lake Huron's quiet waters are perfect for fishing and boating.

But it has no large harbors. No big cities or huge industries disturb its waters. The shores of Lake Huron are quiet and peaceful.

43

To Find Out More

Here are more places where you can explore Lake Huron and the states and provinces around it:

Books

Bonvillain, Nancy. **The Huron.** Chelsea House Publishers, 1989.

Jacobs, William Jay. **La Salle: A Life of Boundless Adventure.** Franklin Watts, 1994.

MacKay, Kathryn. **Ontario.** Children's Press, 1992.

Sirvaitis, Karen. **Michigan.** Lerner Publications, 1994.

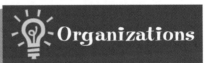

Organizations

Great Lakes Commission
400 Fourth St.
ARGUS II Bldg.
Ann Arbor, MI 48103-4816
(313) 665-9135
glc@glc.org

Michigan Travel Bureau
P.O. Box 30226
Lansing, MI 48909
1-800-5432-YES

Ontario Travel
Queens Park
Toronto, Ontario
Canada M7A 2E5
1-800-ONTARIO

Online Sites

Tour Lake Huron

http://www.great-lakes. net:2200/places/watsheds/ huron/huron.html

Discover the endless attractions of the Great Lakes. This online site has facts about Lake Huron, including information about conservation efforts around the lake.

Visit Ontario, Canada

http://www.great-lakes. net:2200/partners/GLC/pub /circle/ontario.html

On Ontario's Great Lakes and St. Lawrence River shores, you can see wildlife and visit parks and museums.

Explore Michigan

http://www.great-lakes. net:2200/partners/GLC/pub /circle/michigan.html

Wonders can be found in Michigan and the Great Lakes surrounding it. Visit Saginaw Bay, the Straits of Mackinac, white sand beaches, ghost towns, forts, fishing villages, and sparkling cities.

Facts and figures about the Great Lakes

http://www.great-lakes. net:2200/refdesk/almanac/ almanac.html

Includes information about populations and the region.

Important Words

canal man-made waterway for boats

defense protection

democratic to believe that all people are equal

glacier large mass of ice formed when snow piles up and does not melt, often up to 1 mile (1.6 km) deep

measles disease that causes red spots to form on the skin

missionary person who preaches their religion to others

natural resource something used by humans that exists in nature

smallpox disease that causes a fever and skin marks

Index

(**Boldface** page numbers
indicate illustrations.)

Meet the Author

Living in Ohio, close to the Great Lakes, Ann Armbruster pursues her interest in history. A former English teacher and school librarian, she is the author of many books for children.